Cookies, Cakes and Candies

ISBN 0-918831-34-2

U.S. Edition Copyright © 1985 by Gareth Stevens, Inc.

First published in South Africa by Daan Retief Publishers
Copyright © 1983.

U.S. Editor: Joseph F. Westphal
Cover Illustrations: Renée Graef
Typeset by Colony Pre-Press • Milwaukee, WI 53208 USA

Cookies, Cakes and Candies

S.J.A. de Villiers
and
Eunice van der Berg

Illustrated By
Marita Johnson

Gareth Stevens — Milwaukee

First Cookbook Library

Getting Ready To Cook
Drinks and Desserts
One Dish Meals
Vegetables and Salads
Breads and Biscuits
Cookies, Cakes and Candies

These books will show you how easy it is to cook and what fun it is, too.

Everything you have to do is clearly illustrated and the methods you will learn are the same as those used in advanced cookbooks. Once you learn these methods you will be able to follow recipes you find in any cookbook.

This book will show you how to make cookies, cakes and candies. If you follow these recipes you'll be able to create a delicious treat to accompany any meal.

If you are concerned about salt, sugar and fats in your diet, you may reduce the amount called for or substitute other ingredients in many of the recipes. Ask an adult for suggestions.

More information about nutrition, ingredients and cooking methods can be found in GETTING READY TO COOK, a companion volume to this book.

CONTENTS

1. Oatmeal Raisin Cookies 6

2. Chocolate Cookies 8

3. Peanut Butter Cookies 10

4. Vanilla Shortbread 12

5. Coconut Macaroons 14

6. Sugar Cookies 16

7. Fairy Cakes 20

8. Party Cake 24

9. Butter Icing 26

10. Peanut Clusters 27

11. Coconut Fudge 28

12. Nut Caramels 30

Black arrows ➡ in some recipes are reminders to ask a grown-up to help you.

Oatmeal Raisin Cookies

(makes 40 cookies)

Take Out:

2 baking sheets
sieve
mixing bowl
measuring cups
measuring spoons
wooden spoon

knife
chopping board
oven mitts
spatula
cooling rack

What You'll Need

1 cup flour
1 teaspoon salt
1 teaspoon baking soda
1 tablespoon powdered cinnamon
½ cup soft butter or margarine
½ cup brown sugar

⅔ cup white sugar
1 egg
2 tablespoons milk
1 cup seedless raisins
2 cups rolled oats

1. Preheat the oven to 375°.
2. Grease two baking sheets.
3. Sift together the flour, baking soda, and cinnamon into the mixing bowl.

4. Add the butter, sugar, egg, and milk and stir with a wooden spoon. Beat until the mixture is smooth and well blended. You can use a food processor if one is available.

5. Add the raisins and oats and blend well.

6. Use two teaspoons to form lumps of dough and place two inches apart on the baking sheets. Put one baking sheet at a time in the oven for 12 to 15 minutes.

7. Use oven mitts to take the baking sheets from the oven. Place them on the chopping board. Lift the cookies onto the cooling rack with the spatula. Turn off the oven heat.

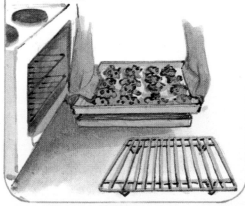

Chocolate Cookies

(to make 40 cookies)

Take Out:

baking sheet
measuring cups
measuring spoons
wooden spoon

saucepan
chopping board
2 teaspoons

What You'll Need

½ cup butter or margarine
2 cups sugar
½ cup cocoa
½ cup milk
3 cups oats
½ cup coconut
1 tablespoon vanilla extract

1. Grease the baking sheet.

2. Measure the butter, sugar, cocoa and milk into the saucepan.

→ 3. Cook the mixture in the saucepan over a medium heat, stirring with a wooden spoon until it starts to boil.

→ 4. Immediately turn the heat to low and let the mixture boil for exactly five minutes. Turn off the heat. Take the saucepan off the burner and put it on the chopping board.

→ 5. Add the oats, coconut and vanilla extract and mix well.

→ 6. Spoon small lumps of the mixture onto the baking sheet with two teaspoons while the mixture is hot.

7. Leave to cool until firm.

Peanut Butter Cookies

(makes 60 cookies)

Take Out:

2 mixing bowls	2 cookie sheets
measuring cups	oven mitts
measuring spoons	chopping board
tablespoon	cooling rack
wooden spoon **or**	fork
electric hand mixer	

What You'll Need

½ cup butter or margarine
½ cup peanut butter
½ cup white sugar
½ cup brown sugar
1 egg
1 ½ cups flour
1 teaspoon baking soda

1. Preheat the oven to 350°. Grease the cookie sheet.

2. Cream the butter and peanut butter in a mixing bowl using the wooden spoon or electric hand mixer.

3. Add the white and brown sugar two spoonfuls at a time. Beat well after each.

4. When all the sugar has been added, beat in the egg. Do not beat after the mixture is well blended.
5. Sift together the flour, salt and baking soda.

6. Stir this mixture gradually into the egg mixture.

7. Knead the dough in the mixing bowl until it is smooth and forms a ball.

8. Roll small round balls of dough in your hands. A heaping tablespoon of dough is enough for each ball.

9. Place the balls about two inches apart in rows on the cookie sheet. Flatten each ball with the fork.

10. Bake each separately for 15 to 20 minutes at a time until the cookies are light brown.

11. Use the oven mitts to take the cookie sheets from the oven and place them on the chopping board. Turn off the oven heat.

12. Use the spatula to place the cookies on the cooling rack to cool.

Vanilla Squares

(makes about 20 squares)

Take Out:

measuring cups
measuring spoons
mixing bowl
wooden spoon
flat baking pan

spatula
fork
knife
chopping board
oven mitts

What You'll Need

½ cup soft butter or margarine
½ cup powdered sugar
¼ cup vanilla pudding mix
1 cup flour
½ teaspoon vanilla extract

1. Preheat the oven to 350°. Grease the baking pan.

2. Measure the butter into the mixing bowl.

3. Add the powdered sugar and pudding mix to the butter. Mix thoroughly and then add the vanilla extract.

4. Add the flour and knead the mixture with your hands until it forms one smooth lump.

5. Press the dough into the baking pan. Smooth the top with the spatula.

6. Prick the dough lightly with a fork.

7. Put the baking pan in the oven for 20 minutes. Use the oven mitts to take it from the oven and place it on the wooden board. Turn off the oven heat.

8. Cut into squares with a knife. Leave them to cool.

9. Use the spatula to lift the squares from the pan into a serving dish.

Coconut Macaroons

(makes 24 cookies)

Take Out:

non-stick cookie sheet
mixing bowl
measuring cups
measuring spoons
fork

2 teaspoons
oven mitts
chopping board
spatula
cooling rack

What You'll Need

1 can sweetened condensed milk (14 ounces)
1 ½ teaspoon vanilla extract
2 ⅓ cups shredded coconut

1. Preheat the oven to 350°.
2. Grease the cookie sheet.

3. Mix everything well in the mixing bowl with a fork.

4. Use the teaspoons to put lumps of the mixture onto the cookie sheet.

5. Bake them for 10 minutes. The tips will turn light brown. Turn off the oven heat.

6. Remove the cookie sheet from the oven with oven mitts. Place it on the chopping board.

7. Lift the coconut macaroons from the baking sheet with the spatula. Leave them to cool on the cooling rack.

Sugar Cookies

(makes 40 cookies)

Take Out:

2 cookie sheets

1 large mixing bowl

1 small mixing bowl

measuring cups

measuring spoons

sieve

pastry blender

egg beater

fork

teaspoon

oven mitts

spatula

chopping board

cooling rack

What You'll Need

3 cups flour

1 cup sugar

½ teaspoon baking soda

¼ teaspoon salt

⅓ cup butter or margarine

1 egg

1½ teaspoons vanilla extract

➡ 1. Preheat the oven to 350°.
2. Grease the cookie sheets.

3. Sift together the flour, sugar, baking soda and salt into the mixing bowl.

4. Add the margarine and rub it into the flour mixture with your fingers or cut it in with the pastry blender. It should look like fine bread crumbs.

5. Beat together the egg and vanilla extract in the small mixing bowl. Add this to the flour mixture and mix with a fork.

6. Knead the dough until it is smooth.

7. Break off about 40 pieces of dough with a teaspoon. Roll them into balls with your hands.

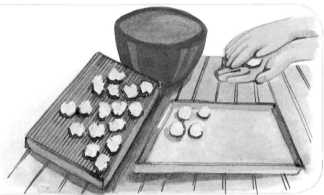

8. The dough can also be formed into figures (see next page), or rolled out with a rolling pin and cut into fancy shapes.

9. Arrange the balls or figures on the baking sheet about three inches apart. Flatten each ball with a teaspoon.

➡ 10. Bake one sheet at a time for 15 minutes. Remove the sheets from the oven and place them on the chopping board.

➡ 11. Lift the cookies from the cookie sheet with the spatula. Allow them to cool on the cooling rack. Turn off the oven heat.

Suggestions for fancy sugar cookies:

Fairy Cakes

(makes 12 to 15)

Take Out:

muffin pan
2 mixing bowls
measuring cups
measuring spoons
wooden spoon **or**
   electric hand mixer
tablespoon

sieve
chopping board
knife
teaspoon
12 to 15 baking cups
oven mitts
cooling rack

What You'll Need

⅓ cup butter or margarine
½ cup sugar
1 teaspoon vanilla extract
1 egg
1 cup flour

¼ teaspoon salt
1 ½ tablespoons baking powder
¼ teaspoon salt
⅓ cup milk
raspberry jam

➡ 1. Preheat the oven to 350°.

2. Place 12 paper baking cups in the muffin pan.

3. Cream the butter in the mixing bowl with the wooden spoon or electric hand mixer.

4. Add three tablespoons sugar at a time and beat thoroughly each time until all the sugar has been used. The mixture must be light and creamy.

5. Add the egg to the butter mixture and beat again to mix well.

6. Sift together the flour, baking powder and salt into the dry mixing bowl.

7. Fold in half the flour mixture into the butter mixture with a tablespoon. Stir in the milk and vanilla.

8. Fold in the rest of the flour mixture carefully until the batter is well blended. It should be a smooth, thick batter.

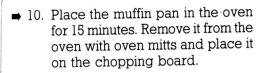

9. Fill the paper cups two-thirds full with the batter, using the table-spoon. Take care not to spill bits of batter around the edges.

10. Place the muffin pan in the oven for 15 minutes. Remove it from the oven with oven mitts and place it on the chopping board.

11. Lift the cakes onto the cooling rack to cool. Turn off the oven heat.

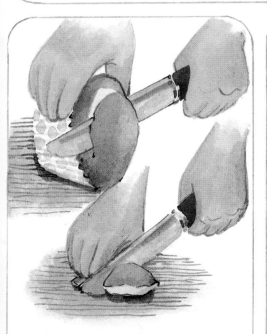

12. Cut off the top of each little cake with the knife. Cut the slice in two halves.

13. Put a teaspoon of jam on each little cake. Place the two half slices back on the jam like two butterfly wings.

Party Cake
(buttercake)

Take Out:

13" x 9" x 3" pan
2 mixing bowls
measuring cups
measuring spoons
wooden spoon **or**
   electric hand mixer
tablespoon

tablespoon
sieve
plastic scraper
oven mitts
chopping board
knife
cooling rack

What You'll Need

½ cup butter or margarine
1 cup sugar
1 teaspoon vanilla extract
2 eggs
2 cups flour

1 tablespoon baking powder
½ teaspoon salt
⅔ cup milk
butter icing (see page 26)
jelly beans and jimmies

1. Preheat the oven to 350°.
2. Grease the cake pan.
3. Follow the instructions for fairy cakes (page 20) from step 3 to step 8.

9. Turn the batter into the greased cake pan. Scrape all the batter from the mixing bowl with a plastic scraper. Spread evenly on top.

10. Bake the cake for 25 minutes. When the cake is done it will shrink away from the side of the pan. Remove it from the oven with oven mitts and place it on the chopping board. Turn off the oven heat.

11. Run a knife along the sides of the cake to loosen it from the pan. Turn it out onto the cooling rack. Leave it to cool completely.

12. Spread the cake with butter icing using a knife. Decorate it with jelly beans and jimmies.

Butter Icing

(to ice a cake or cookies)

Take Out:

measuring cups
measuring spoons
2 small mixing bowls
sieve
wooden spoon **or**
   electric hand mixer
plastic scraper
knife

What You'll Need

3 tablespoons soft butter or margarine
1 ⅓ cup powdered sugar

2 ½ teaspoons milk
1 teaspoon vanilla extract

1. Sift the powdered sugar into the mixing bowl.

2. Measure the butter into the other mixing bowl.

3. Beat the butter with the wooden spoon or electric hand mixer. Add one cup of powdered sugar gradually.

4. Beat in the milk and vanilla extract. Add the remaining powdered sugar and beat until the icing is light and creamy. Add one more teaspoon milk if the icing is too thick to spread.

5. Spread the butter icing on the cake or cookies with a knife.

Peanut Clusters

(makes 20)

Take Out:
cookie sheet
small double boiler
fork
2 teaspoons

What You'll Need

4 ounces milk chocolate
4 ounces roasted peanuts

1. Grease the cookie sheet.
➡ 2. Turn on a burner to medium.
➡ 3. Pour two cups hot water into the bottom half of the double boiler. Put it on the hot burner.
➡ 4. Break the chocolate into the top of the double boiler.

➡ 5. Slowly melt the chocolate over the hot water. Remove the top half of the double boiler immediately when the chocolate has melted.

➡ 6. Stir the peanuts into the chocolate with the fork. Mix well.

➡ 7. Use two teaspoons to drop the peanut clusters onto the greased cookie sheet. Work rapidly while the chocolate is still hot. Leave to cool.

Coconut Fudge

(makes about 60 squares)

Take Out:

measuring cups
measuring spoons
saucepan
wooden spoon
plastic scraper

flat pan (8″ x 12″)
chopping board
knife
serving plate

What You'll Need

3 cups sugar
¼ teaspoon salt
1 cup cream
½ cup moist, shredded coconut
1 teaspoon vanilla extract

1. Grease the pan.

2. Measure the sugar, salt, and cream into the saucepan.

➡ 3. Turn on the burner to medium. Place the saucepan on the heat and stir the mixture with the wooden spoon until the sugar has dissolved.

➡ 4. Add the coconut to the sugar mixture. Let it boil for 10 minutes. Stir occasionally with the wooden spoon. Turn off the heat.

➡ 5. Remove the saucepan from the stove and put it on the chopping board. Stir in the vanilla.

➡ 6. Stir the fudge with the wooden spoon until it starts to thicken.

➡ 7. Scrape the fudge into the greased pan with the plastic scraper and level on top.

8. Leave to cool completely. Cut the coconut fudge into squares and lift them onto the serving plate with the knife.

Nut Caramels

(makes about 60 caramels)

Take Out:

flat pan (8" x 8")
sieve
mixing bowl
saucepan
measuring cups

measuring spoons
wooden spoons
tablespoon
knife
chopping board

What You'll Need

2 cups powdered sugar
½ cup butter or margarine
1 cup brown sugar
¼ cup milk
1 cup broken walnuts or pecans
1 teaspoon vanilla extract

1. Grease the oven pan.
2. Sift the powdered sugar into the mixing bowl.
3. Measure the butter and brown sugar into the saucepan.

→ 4. Turn the burner to low heat and put the saucepan on it.

→ 5. Stir constantly with the wooden spoon while the butter and sugar melt together. Let it boil for two minutes. Stir continuously.

→ 6. Stir in the milk. Keep on stirring until it boils again. Turn off the heat.

→ 7. Remove the saucepan from the stove and put it on the chopping board. Leave it to cool until lukewarm.

8. Beat powdered sugar into the butter mixture, a little at a time.

9. Add the nuts and vanilla extract. Stir until it thickens.

10. Scrape the mixture into the greased pan and level the top with the tablespoon.

11. Put it in the refrigerator to cool. Cut the caramels into squares.

INDEX

B
Butter icing 26

C
Cake, party 24
Cakes, fairy 20
Caramels, nut 30
Chocolate cookies 8
Clusters, peanut 27
Coconut fudge 28
Coconut macaroons 14
Cookies, chocolate 8
Cookies, oatmeal raisin 6
Cookies, peanut butter 10
Cookies, sugar 16

F
Fairy cakes 20
Fudge, coconut 28

I
Icing, butter 26

M
Macaroons, coconut 14

N
Nut caramels 30

O
Oatmeal raisin cookies 6

P
Party cake 24
Peanut butter cookies 10
Peanut clusters 27

S
Squares, vanilla 12
Sugar cookies 16

V
Vanilla squares 12

Black arrows ➡ in some recipes are reminders to ask a grown-up to help you.